How I Got Over

Jan F. Whitaker

Unless otherwise indicated, scriptural quotations are taken from the King James Version of the Bible.

Dedication

This book is dedicated to all the hurting people throughout this nation. I want each of you to know God has a plan for your life. This book was written more than just merely to tell the story of my life. But it was written to empower people's lives. It was written to empower the minds and hearts of individuals who have experienced disappointments and discouragements in their lives whether it is personal, spiritual, or otherwise.

This book was also designed to help you better understand the love of the Father and His mercy that He shows toward humanity. This book will strengthen your walk with Him and if by chance you do not know the Father God, all you have to do is ask Him to come into your life and let His Holy Spirit dwell and abide inside of you.

Perhaps, there maybe some who will read this book and say they have not been through anything. I encourage these individuals to *"just keep on living..."* Life has a way of humbling and challenging us all. Believe me, you **will** experience some things in your life. However, you will discover; though, if you serve God that He can bring you out of anything, just like He did for me. Inside of this book you will hear some of my testimonies as they relate to my many life's struggles and "How I Got Over."

You see, there are no guarantees or extended warranties that will last in this lifetime. And many have a tendency to put their trust in all the worldly things such as warranties and guarantees from people and things. For instance, when we purchase a new vehicle, we purchase a warranty, believing that our vehicle will be protected when something happens to it. But, I am here to inform you there is always a catch to anything that is man-made. The only real and sure guarantee in this life is to follow Christ Jesus.

Even though the road has not been easy, I have learned and believed that God is the source of my strength, and that God will always stand behind all of His guarantees, warranties, and promises. Although the tears, pain and depression were very real for me, God extended His hand to me, and healed me only when I decided to give my whole heart to Him and accept those things that I could not change.

I have found that the hardest person in the world for me to deal with is me. I could give everyone else sound advice about issues regarding their life, and it would work well for them. But when it came to me, I couldn't properly deal with the problem. I thank God for bringing me out of the darkness into the His Marvelous Light.

I would also like to offer a special

thanks to some people who have been very instrumental in my life. First and foremost I thank God for Jesus. I'd also like to thank my four wonderful boys: Roderick, Jeremy, Cameron and Korey Whitaker. Nan E. Turner, who was my childhood role model and still is to this day; and Pastor Eddie and Brenda Giles who took me under their wings. I thank Kay and Mike Asher for their ongoing support, positive encouraging words, laughter, and just for being there when I needed them no matter what. Thanks to all of my wonderful brothers and sisters for their continued support and to a host of other family members and friends. To Pastor Michael and Corine Bowman — thank you for your love and support. I even want to thank my enemies because they helped keep me before God on my knees, *and they still do to this very day.*

I thank God for each of you, for without God sending you into my life I could not have fulfilled one of His many purposes and the mission that He ordained for my life which is to help others.

Table of Contents

CHAPTER ONE

I Dreamed the Dream

In 1995, God spoke to me (in a still audible voice) about writing a book concerning the accounts of my life. Immediately, He gave me the title, "How I Got Over."

I was so excited that I shared it with my mentor and best friend, Kay Asher. Since this time, Kay and her husband, Mike have played a tremendous part in birthing this book into existence. I would talk with them about all that God wanted me to do and my plans for the book. They would be so thrilled and excited. You would have thought they were writing the book. Also, they were always available to help.

I also had two other dear friends, Juanita Harbor and Lisa Myers that I entrusted this with.

They stood by me through thick and thin. And even though I knew they grew tired and weary of hearing and reading excerpts of this book, and all the other drama that came along with publishing it, they never gave up on me. They listened to my frustrations and all my other insecurities. But most of all, their patience is to be commended. They always had a positive word and said, I could do it. They are true friends and Saints of God, for only real Christians would make the sacrifices that they did for another and stick by them to the very end with no complaints.

Anyway...on with the story... All of this sounded good except I felt as though I was not spiritually ready and was certainly not ready to talk about my life, let alone disclose all the painful details to total strangers. *Now isn't this something. We can find every excuse in the book sometimes not to do God's Will, even when we know He spoke to us?*

So, I procrastinated. I did not believe that I was spiritually prepared to live up to the task that God had placed before me to write this book. Fear was controlling my life. The Bible says God has not given us the spirit of fear, but power, love and a sound mind (2 Timothy 1:7). At that time in my life I allowed Satan and many of life's circumstances to shape my future and dictate my life. Also, I was still running from my calling and had not completely given up all the things of the world.

I was like so many today that are struggling with totally surrendering their life and will to Him. I was too saved to be classified as a sinner and I was too much of a sinner to be completely classified as a Christian. When I look back over my life and at some of the things I did, I can hardly believe I did these things. I am truly remorseful for all the bad and insensitive things I have done and all the times I walked out of the will of God. So as I share my story with you, remember to stay focused on the message and not the messenger.

One of the biggest strongholds I had to struggle with in my life for numerous years was with gambling. I used to gamble at the racetrack and the casino, everywhere and anywhere I went, 5 to 7 days a week. I was so vexed and consumed with gambling that even after going to church, this was the only thing that would be on my mind. So I would head to the races. The Word of God says you can't serve two master; for either he would hate the one, and love the other, or else he would hold to one and despise the other, ye cannot serve God and mammon (Matthew 6:24). It is obvious now that gambling was my god and not the almighty God.

However, one of the strangest things to me was that I never lost money when I gambled. And when I say *never* in this situation, I truly mean never. In hindsight, I now know that even though I did not lose money, I was headed in the direction of losing the blessings of God. You may be curious and ask the question, "How was I going to lose my blessings from God?" Well, I'm so glad you asked.

The Word of God plainly says for us to "Trust in the Lord with all thine heart, and lean not unto thy own understanding. In all thy ways acknowledge Him and He shall direct thy path" (Proverbs 3:5-6). To me this scripture says it all. God wants us to trust and depend on Him for everything, not just some things. I recall making excuses to myself to keep on gambling. I said this helps me forget about my problems as well as make them seem non-existence.

But let me enlighten you about the whole truth. Whatever method you use to tackle your problem(s); if it's not God's method it is an ineffective mean, and you will lose every time. As I reflect back over my life, I can recall how I allowed other people, especially those who were close to me and whom I had believed to have my best interest at heart, to say things to me like, "Jan, you've got to have some type of fun/recreation or you'll go crazy." Satan knew my weakness as well as my strengths and he used people to prey upon them. He knew that I was and am highly favored of God and that God had a plan for my life.

Satan's goal was to keep me from the real truth about God and to keep me from the purpose and destiny that God had ordained for me before the foundation of the earth, and before I was formed in my mother's womb.

Satan comes to kill, steal, and destroy. As you read this book, you will find out just how Satan can use his tactics and tricks to destroy lives. You will find out how he will use them to destroy your life just like he did with Eve in the Garden concerning The Tree of Life. If you have not learned how to outwit the devil, just know that the Word of God says that Jesus was manifested that He might destroy the works of the devil (I John 3:8). The Word has been out for decades and I want to inform some and update others that Jesus is a man of war, and the only sure weapon is the Word of God.

We must eat, sleep, live and believe God's Word. We must stay focus and read the Word daily, so we will be able to hear God's still small voice when He is speaking. We don't want to end up like Jacob in Genesis 28, when he went to sleep and woke up and said, "Surely, the Lord has been in this place and I knew it not." We want to know His voice.

Now remember, God speaks to everyone differently and He has wonderfully made us all. We are all uniquely crafted. Don't let anyone turn you away from God. For His way is the only way. God's Word says, "I am the Way, the Truth, and the Life; no man cometh unto the Father except by me" (John 14:6).

Now let me share how even more pathetic I was with gambling. People can justify just about anything they want to do. When I think about what I did with my winnings, I know now it was a crutch to compensate for an addiction. I would take my winnings and help mothers who needed assistance with purchasing diapers, milk, et cetera for their babies. I would also help people who said they were hungry. I would help my parents and family or just about anyone who said they needed it.

But in all of this I was not properly using the gifts that God gave me to discern the tricks of the enemy. The rationale I used to keep on gambling was that God allowed me to win, so I could help others. I am reminded of one specific incident where some of my family members called from out of town, and said they would come down to see me, but they didn't have the money. I would encourage them anyway because I knew I could gamble and win some money to give them. Needless to say, I would, and when they arrived I would have at least $100 to $200 dollars to give them. But I know better than this now. Listen carefully! God never ordained gambling as a means of helping others.

God gave me gifts and I abused them at that time simply because I did not know any better. But, guess what? When we learn better, we should do better. I did not realize back then that God was molding and shaping my life. So, due to my lack of understanding, I almost missed my blessings. The Word of God says, "In all of your getting, get understanding" (Proverbs 4:7).

As I tell my story, I sincerely pray that you will see and understand "How I Got Over." This book is a power pack account of my past struggles, both natural and spiritual, with special emphasis on the verbal, mental and physical abuse I experienced. And because I did not effectively deal with them, the struggles eventually led to depression and other symptoms.

As you read this book, you will see an account of how I carried much of the pain that was inside of me until I was older. Because I was not properly equipped and did not understand then how to put on the whole armor of God to stand against the wiles of the devil (Ephesians 6:11), it almost destroyed me.

As a child, I grew up in a loving Christian home. When you come from that kind of home and then go into a home of endless hidden abuse and you don't use God's weapons to stand, the devil will attempt to destroy you. Like the old adage says, "He will chew you up and spit you out," and have the nerve to move on to someone else when he believes his goal has been accomplished. So remember, you always need to have faith in God — put His Word inside of you on a daily basis. Stay prayed up, believe in Jesus' death, burial, and resurrection and; therefore, you will know that you are covered under God's blood. However, if you chose to do it your way then consider yourself "dead meat" for Satan to destroy you for you have given him an open invitation to your life.

CHAPTER TWO

My Childhood Years: Feelings Don't Count With God

During my childhood years, I was a very sensitive child. Even the minute things would hurt my feeling. I was always taught to be kind to others, and for the majority of the time, I tried to practiced this teaching. But I quickly learned just because you are nice and kind to someone it doesn't mean that it would be reciprocated. The Word of God says to pray for them which **despitefully use you** (Luke 6:28). So, based on this scripture I would choose to suffer personally before hurting anyone in any way.

So, I struggled with the pain of being criticized and rejected by others most of my life. People took my kindness and meekness for weakness.

Even to this day, the pain that were afflicted upon me are still very real and prevalent in my life. One of the reasons I believe this has happened is because I know God has chosen me and the enemy has tried to discourage me throughout my life by using other people to hurt me.

The Word of God says when we render good for evil it will heap coals of fire on our enemies' head (Proverbs 25:22). No matter how someone treats you, always remember your response must be in accordance with the Word of God. We are called to emulate Christ not other people. This means if a person does not possess a Christ-like attitude or if what they are doing or saying does not line up with God's Word, then you should not be inclined to follow them.

If you believe someone has mistreated you or taken advantage of you, consider these promises and encouraging words from God. First of all, what you're going through is only for a season and this too shall pass. "Fret not yourself because of evildoers for they shall soon be cut down like the grass and whither as the green herbs" (Psalm 37:1-2).

No matter what people do to you, you should continue to show them kindness from your heart, not superficial, but a genuine response. We have to be real with it. God do not honor deceit and dishonesty from anyone. God only honors truth.

Trust the Word of God for He promises to never leave you alone (Hebrews 13:5). If, in God's eyes, your heart is right, you will always come out a winner and on top. Remember, everyone who says they love the Lord doesn't always mean it. For some they are just idle words, with no personal conviction within their hearts. I truly believe if they knew who they really were and how God really loves them, their confession will no longer be just idle words, but they would be sincere and coming from the heart.

There are many scriptures in the Word of God that people have used to continue in sin. For example: "We all have sinned, and come short of His Glory (Romans 3:23)." But when will we stop hiding behind scriptures like these to justify our wrongdoings? When will we get off the MILK and get to the MEAT of God's Word and what God is really all about?

When Jesus walked upon this earth, He was about His Father's business. As believers, we are called to do the same. Our focus must be on winning lost souls to Him instead of losing souls because of our ungodly behaviors.

Christians who operate out of a ungodly nature — hurting people deliberately are not true examples of what a Christian should be like. When I encounter people like this, I know I am dealing with a religious person and not a person that have a true relationship with God. They are what some call, "Sunday Christians." Jesus called these types of people lukewarm and hypocrites. They only have a tendency to call on the name of Jesus when they need something from Him.

Isn't it funny how when things are going real bad in people' lives how they are able to recognize and honor God relentlessly. They confess how they are going to do better and how they want to live for Jesus. How they are going to go to church every Sunday. But as soon as God deliver them through their trials, they return to their old sinful ways. I have seen this happened repeatedly.

There will always be people in society that will challenge that which you know to be true. Many of whom "says" they are saved. But in their hearts they know they are not. But nevertheless, we cannot let these kinds of people and attitudes discourage us and cause us to act vengefully. Vengeance is something God is in control of, "vengeance is Mine" and "I will repay" (Romans 12:19).

Remember, we have a Father who sits high and looks low. He guides us and leads us. The Psalmist says, "The steps of a good man are ordered by the Lord" (Psalm 37:23). And when we don't understand some things, guess what? We have a Heavenly Father who does understand. We can then say with confidence, I'm so glad trouble doesn't last always. So when answers just don't come, don't be discouraged. Keep on leaning on God's steadfast love and trusting in His word. If you really think about it, knowing really doesn't make that much of a difference. But growing close and knowing Jesus, will. Let me encourage you to be more than "a one day of a week" Christian. Be determine in your heart to serve Him everyday.

I have not always understood what God was doing in my life, but I now know that He was trying to mold, shape and prepare me to be used for His glory for such a time as this. He was preparing me to be one of His twenty-first century disciples. My momma and I would often have some private conversations about things that I believed I was suffering with. This is what I called it at that time. I was very careful and discreet not to let others know what we were talking about. As far as my mother goes, she was the best secret keeper. So I knew she would hold these things dear to her heart and never repeat them. Looking back over my life, I can see that God had endowed me with alot of wisdom even at a young age. Somehow I knew that everything was not to be shared with everybody. Some people's minds are not ready for some things.

But knowing this and acting upon it was two different things. So, sometimes when God would speak to me, I would run and share it with others. What I found out, though, when I did this it would cause a delay in God's plan for my life. The reason I would do this is because I thought I could trust them. After all they were my family and friends.

This was an ongoing lesson in my life. God kept giving me chance after chance to learn to trust only in Him. The Word of God says to "Trust in the Lord with all thine heart and lean not unto thy own understanding" (Proverbs 3:5). It also tells us to "seek ye first the kingdom of God and His righteousness and all these things shall be added unto you" (Matthew 6:33).

Remember as I said earlier in this book, during my early years I was experiencing an enormous amount of fear in regards to the gifts and talents that God had placed inside of me. And since there were so many who referred to me as literally being crazy, I sometimes acted out or portrayed the part.

The book of Ephesians tells us that we wrestle not against flesh and blood, but against principalities, powers, rulers of darkness of this world and spiritual wickedness in high places (Ephesians 6:12). People are flesh and blood and when people allow the devil to operate through them by lashing out at others with their tongues anything can come out of their mouths.

God wonderfully made us and He loves us all unconditionally, regardless of what anyone else may think or believe. It says in His Word that God so loved the world that He gave His only begotten Son that whosoever believeth in Him shall not perish, but have everlasting life (John 3:16). Now "ain't" that good news? I ask you, how many of you would be willing to sacrifice your son or anyone close to you to save another?

You know, I have found in my experiences that everything in the world can be funny to others when it deals with someone else. But when it happens to them, then everything changes because the "shoe is on the other foot." When it happens to them it no longer feels good. I have also been guilty of doing this also. I have laughed at jokes about other people when they were going through things. But I did not understand at that time that even though you are not the one that is telling the jokes, you are just as guilty for listening to it. So here's a piece of advice that I want to share with you. Be careful about the words you say each day, and keep them few and sweet for you don't know from day to day which ones you'll have to eat (Proverbs 18).

The only person that I believed really understood me and my pain during this time was my mother. It is said that a mother loves at all times. This depicts my mother's sentiment definitively. My father was also an important part of my life, but so often he had to be away from home because of his work. Regardless, family was first.

I recall feeling very special because I grew up in a family where love was unconditional. Yes, we had our ups and downs, but the love we felt for each other outweighed all of the problems. I grew up in a home with four brothers and three sisters. Four of which is older than myself. Actually I am the middle child.

Can you imagine the drama that my parents had to deal with on a daily basis? I know that I was a handful all by myself. But guess what? I never heard them complain. They would fuss and teach us right from wrong. But I never heard my parents say anything negative about our family. My parents were by no means perfect. They were like so many other parents who made everyday life's mistakes. But they worked hard to prepare us for the challenges of life and provided a Christian atmosphere in our home.

My mother did not send us to church, she took us to church. Every time the church doors opened, we were there. I recalled once telling my youngest sister that when I grow up, I was not going to attend church. But guess what? Church was one of the first places I wanted to be. The Word of God says to train up a child in the way you would have them to go and when he is old he will not depart from it (Proverbs 22:6).

You know how we allow society to dictate that girls need to learn certain life's tasks like, for instance, cooking. Well, I never really learned how to cook. I had that special way of charming my daddy when I didn't want to do something. He would do it for me if it was within reason. *Even though I was always called a daddy's girl, I spent most of my time with my mother.*

I would also talk my daddy into letting me ride with he and my brothers when they would go out in the truck to cut firewood for the chimney. I always knew that my daddy was going to get me some *"old-fashion bar-be-que,"* so I would always ask to go. We would eat it before returning home because I thought my other siblings wouldn't know about it. But still I think they had an idea; for daddy would always take some home. Anyway, many say that I am spoiled, but the truth is I'm not.

I received Jesus and was baptized at age nine. I immediately started to work in the church. I did anything…teaching classes, presiding as Sunday School Superintendent, even singing in the choir. I became very popular as a lead singer. I always loved to sing. Even to this day. I used to pick up bottles or anything that I could use and pretend that it was my microphone. My daddy and mother also loved to sing.

In the early stages of my life when I was participating in the church, though, I did not have a kingdom agenda. But I thank God for His mercy and grace. Because He knew my heart in spite of this.

When we receive Christ into our lives, we place ourselves in a position to be molded and shaped into whatever God wants us to be. So, even though we are saved, God is still working on us. The only difference is that God is living in us. Let's get even more real with this. Some people will try to make you think that you can't be saved and that God doesn't love you because their sin was less than yours. But again, guess what? They are a lair and this is not the truth. God can save us all if we want to be saved. You see it is not our goodness or niceness that turned our lives around. It is God that changes people's lives. We are saved by grace through faith. Salvation is something we have not earned on our own. It is a gift from God.

Some of us want to make getting saved so hard, but those are the religious folk. Remember, if you can believe on God, that little bit will cause your life to be enriched. So, I ask you the question, do you have a "But God Story?" Well, if you don't yet, just keep living and watch it come to pass. For the Word of God says that every knee shall bow and every tongue shall confess to God (Romans 14:11).

CHAPTER THREE

A Mother's & Daddy's Love: There's No Greater Love Than God's

Now, I believe that a real mother loves her children unconditionally. At least this is the way I thought about my mom. My momma was a praying woman. I always use to hear her praying to God and singing those old 100 hymnals as we call them. The ones like "I KNOW I AM A CHILD OF GOD" and "FATHER I STRETCH MY HANDS TO THEE NO OTHER HELP I KNOW." I would talk to my momma about all of my innermost thoughts. I could tell her anything and she always seemed to understand me and make things all better.

I am reminded of talking to her about what I called at that time of hearing voices in my head, acting strange, being able to feel others' pain, and seeing things before they actually happened. My momma would hug me and say to me, "Baby that's God talking to you." Well surely I did not understand what she was talking about, so she tried to explain to a young child the best she knew how.

I recalled her telling me that I was chosen of God and He has picked me out from among others to do His works. Well, even though I did not understand this, I believed it simply because my momma said it, and I was okay with this until some children at school started making fun of me and calling me strange. Can't children be mean sometimes?

There were even some older people that called themselves "Christians" in the church, so called friends, and enemies that called me strange and ridiculed and mocked me. As a result of their selfishness, I would cry, and try to hide behind my momma and daddy in an effort to make it all go away and for them to leave me alone. But again, guess what? It did not work. For I had not learned completely how to lean and depend on Jesus for myself.

Regardless, my mother and daddy would always tell me not to worry and that everything would be all right. I recalled thinking that if I could give them my gifts (being able to see things ahead of time and feeling people's pain) that they would feel special, too and my problems would disappear. But I needed to put my trust in God instead of man. Psalm 46:1 says it this way, God is a very present help in the time of trouble.

When we are going through things, we need to keep in mind that we are not responsible for how others treat us. However we are held accountable for how we treat others. The Word of God explains that "we shalt love the Lord thy God with all thy heart, and with all thy soul, and with all thy strength" and that "thou shalt love thy neighbor as thyself" (Mark 12:30-31). Now in order to do this, you will need to follow two simple principles: love God and love others.

When you let go and love God totally and care for others as you do yourself, then and only then can you fulfill the laws of what the Ten Commandments and Old Testaments laws commands us to do. Jesus says these two Commandments summarize all God's laws. We have to allow these laws to rule our thoughts, decisions and actions. Remember, anytime you are uncertain about what to do, ask yourself what course of action demonstrates God's love for others.

Let me also tell you that a real daddy's love never ends either, even though society has a tendency to focus more on a mother's love. I want you to know that there are some wonderful daddies in the world as well. I know from experience because I had one.

My daddy and I use to sit and he would talk to me about the "birds and the bees and the flowers and the trees, and the moon up above and a thang called love," just as my mother did. My daddy always had his children's best interest at heart, especially his girls. He tried to protect us from all those so call "big bad wolves." I know that there are some readers that can relate to what I am saying. When you have a real daddy they are one in a million. Now my daddy was not without faults, but he was truly a daddy in every sense of the word. He provided for his family and he and my mother fed everyone else's children as well as anyone that came around.

I remember when I made the basketball team in the sixth grade and how proud my daddy was of me. My daddy would make all of his children feel so special; especially when we received any type of award for whatever reasons. My daddy would always be right there cheering us on. By the way, my daddy loved to sing the blues. During those years, I enjoyed them as well.

Oh! One of the most exciting times in my life was when my daddy landed a part in a movie that played at all the theaters in the early 70's. My daddy starred with Vic Morrow and Karen Black in the movie titled, "The Evictors;" which was produced by Paramount Pictures. This was an awesome time to see our daddy on the big screen at the movies. In the movie he dies, and I remember asking him about how they made it seemed so real and if they use ketchup for blood. He explained that they have so many special effects in the movies and that it is always something new and innovative.

Now when I would get in trouble with my daddy I knew if I could outwit him. I would be okay because eventually he would forget it. But on the other hand, my mother was totally different. If you ran from her, she would not even attempt to run behind you, she would wait until you go to bed and get one of those switches off the Channy Berry Tree and whip you.

I recall that I got more whipping more then I care to think about. I would scream and holler like she was killing me or something. *(You know how we "play fake" sometime to get our own way).* Anyway, if my daddy was home, he would come in and say to my momma, "Don't hurt that gal," even though I was getting what I deserved. She knew I had gotten smart enough to know that if I yelled loud enough my daddy would persuade her to stop. Oh, yes, I had this little trick down pat. Proverbs 13:24 says if you spare the rod, you will spoil the child. I can tell you that my parents did not spare the rod. I was just a daddy's girl and managed to get away with a few things.

Like I said earlier, when we learn better, we should do better. My parents demonstrated and taught us love for each other as well as for others. I'll say it this way in my momma words, "It's nice to be nice.' These words will linger in my heart forever.

CHAPTER FOUR

My Teenage Years

My teenage years is what I called my drama years. My parents had to deal with so much craziness from me during this time in my life. If there was ever was a period in my life that I rejected the purpose and plan of God for my life was during these years.

I was determine to be a part of the "in crowd." So, I hung around with this group and that group. I didn't want to feel unpopular. But no matter what I did, I did not fit in. When you are mark for kingdom business and purpose, you will never fit into the world system.

Let me tell you this, being unpopular can be a good thing sometimes. But even though I hung with the wrong crowd at times, I never forsook going to church.

Going to church, however, for me during these years was not the same as serving God. I can tell you right now, if you don't have an open mind to receive from God; then don't expect anything from God. Because when you go to church like this, you will end up leaving in the same condition that you came. The Word of God tells us that faith cometh by hearing and hearing by the Word of God (Romans 10:17). So, whatever we do in all our getting, we must get understanding (Proverbs 4:7).

Now, even though God placed inside of me gifts and talents at an early age, because of my lack of understanding of God's Word, "I could not see the forest for the trees." In other words, I was only focused on the natural worldly circumstances for I was still not ready for God to use me due to the lack of knowledge that God is the very source of my very being and strength. I had not learned how to trust in the Lord with all my heart and lean not to my own understanding (Proverbs 3:5). You see, it does not matter how much momma and daddy teach you or how much you go to church. If you don't get the Word of God inside of you, no one else can plant it in you and make it grow. You'll have to grow for yourself.

Now, my teenage years were not without disappointments as well as struggles. First of all like all average American families, I bickered and argued with my brothers and sister at times. We were smart enough to know, though, that we did not want to make it a habit because our parents did not put up with up fighting and arguing with each other. This was a high priority on their taboo list. Now, if you have ever been whipped with a "switch," you would do everything in your power to stay away from trouble.

I am reminded of one of the times I was supposed to have washed the dishes and I didn't. I already knew I was in trouble, so when my mother got home she called me and asked me about it and I ran from my mother to my daddy. Now my mother, unlike my daddy, never ran after anyone. But, oh boy, she would wait patiently until you think she had forgotten. To my amazement, she made one of her bedtime appointment. She waited until I got in the bed and began to whip me. I could feel the licks from the switches all the way through my pajamas. But some-times when I was planning to do something that might warrant a whipping, I would wait until I knew my daddy was coming home, so he could intervene. Most of the times my daddy could talk my momma out of whipping me depending on how serious the act of wrongdoing was.

In my family I had two brothers and two sisters that were older than me. Because I had older siblings, life did not seem so hard for me as I imagined it was for them. I recalled during the time that I was still in high school that my two oldest brothers went off to the military to serve their country. They would send money home to my parents to help in an attempt to make life better for us.

I believe we all have someone we look up to in our family. Now, I love all of my brothers and sisters, but I always looked up to my oldest brother and still do to this day. He always seemed to have the right answers and took the time to show me how to do things the right way. He also taught me how to drive.

My brother has a 442 Oldsmobile, which inci-dentally was a stick shift. I remember being told that if you can't drive a stick shift you don't really know how to drive. Well, if you know anything about cars, you would remember back in the seventies the five speeds did not have the same type of shifts that the newer vehicles have now. The shifts back then were much longer. Anyway, my brother took me out on the highway in our country town of Holly, Louisiana for the first time. He started me out on a dirt road. I am sure some of you all can relate to the dirt roads. I was so happy that I had advanced to the highway. And I was so excited that my brother trusted me enough to let me practice driving his new car. I drove well down the road, but then it was time to back up and turn around. I attempted to back up and let off the clutch too fast and the car stopped in the highway. Believe it or not, we looked up and a big 18-wheeler was coming towards us very fast. My brother thought quickly as usual and removed me from under the wheel and got the car out of the street. We survived this little episode, and believe it or not, my brother still continued to teach me how to drive.

Now on to my next oldest brother who fought in the Vietnam war. I begged him to let me drive his car when I was a senior in high school and he did. He told me not to take the car anywhere but to school. But you know how it is sometime with teenagers. We have a tendency to only hear what we want to hear. I thought that I was Ms. Big Stuff driving my brother's car. So on that same day all my friends and I decided we would go to the store and no one would know. We did get permission from the Principal, but my brother had told me just to drive to school and no place else. Well, we left school and went to the store.

So, on our way back, I was driving too fast trying to get back to school and hit a hole in the road coming around a curve and lost control of the car and ended up in a ditch. Now, you have heard the saying that God takes care of old folks and fools. Well, that's the way we felt at that time. We all felt like fools. Through God's grace and mercy we all ended up safe. But isn't it strange about how we can thank God in one breath and lie in another to get our own selfish way? Well, we all checked the damage out on the car and it was not too bad. You could not see the dent well unless you paid very close attention when walking toward the car. We decided to not tell my brother, so I could get the car again.

We got some help and they pulled the car out of the ditch and cleaned it up. The dent was deceiving, just as we were. Well, oddly enough we pulled it off for years, until finally one day we were all in a conversation, and my brother was present, and one of the persons who was with us at the time, let the "cat out of the bag" as some of the old folk say. You see what we thought was a harmless little lie at the time came back to haunt us years later. My momma and grandma always told me that what you do in the dark will always come to the light. They also said if you tell one lie, you got to keep on telling them, so it is always best to tell the truth. We soon found out in the Word of God that the truth would make us free (John 8:32). Thank you Jesus!!

I began playing basketball in the sixth grade and made the basketball team when I got in high school as well. I believed that I was good, for to make the team you have to have the right stuff to qualify along with the right moves and good shooting power. I was so thankful that I possessed the talent. I was kind of beside myself as some of the older people put it. My daddy was so proud of me and I was excited, as I had accomplished a skill that some other did not possess. The Word of God says that I can do all things through Christ who strengthen me (Philippians 4:13). During the time I played we won the State championship two times and brought home a trophy from other tournaments that I played in. The Word of God says ask and it shall be given to you; seek and you shall find; knock and it shall be open unto you (Luke 11:9). If you ask anything in his name, it shall be given unto you. My parents always taught us we could do anything that we put our minds to and that if we believe it in our hearts, we can achieve it. I went on to graduate from Second Ward High School.

CHAPTER FIVE

My College Years and Married Years

After my graduation from high school, I went on to college to fulfill my childhood dreams and my parents'. The only career I ever wanted was to be a school teacher. So upon my high school graduation, I went to college.

My parents were very strict on us growing up. I recall that my mother had my brother to take me and picked me up from my junior/senior prom. I remembered being so disappointed and upset because I wanted to go with the guy I was dating. It was in the 12th grade that I began dating, and I met this wonderful guy. He attended another high school in the area, so I wanted him to take me to the prom. My parents, however, had other plans. Believe it or not, teenagers, my parents knew what was best for me.

Teenagers, for some reason have a tendency not to listen to their parents. But let me enlighten you and let you know that your parents do know what's best for you, even if you don't believe it. Anyway, I got through the drama of my brother taking me to my prom, and when I look back on it, I know that it was as bad for him as it was for me.

You know how we are in the flesh and not in the spirit at times. And we can end up with just about anything. Everything that looks good is not always the best thing for you. Take it from me. I was married twice, and in both of my marriages, I chose the men myself. God did not instruct me to marry them. As a matter of fact, I forgot all about God.

Let me be real with you about God's Word. I was looking at the outer man and not at the heart. All the charming words that came out of their mouths were just what a woman would want to hear. But I now know that God did not join me together in either one of my marriages.

During my first marriage, my husband and I prospered very quickly, meaning that we had everything anyone could want from a materialistic viewpoint. God gave us four wonderful boys, two homes, new cars every two years, plus money. Sounds good, huh!!

Well, this "perfect" marriage did not work out. I prayed 24-7 for my marriage to work. I was not sure how to pray, but I was real about what I was saying. I chose to stay with my husband because I believed that since I had stood before God and said my vows, it was my duty to stay with him no matter what. Plus, he made me feel so guilty all the time. So, like any good mother, I just wanted the children to be with their father. All of the wrong reasons, if God did not ordain it. You see "things," and all the money in the world, do not make you happy if you are not with the mate God purposed for you.

If you think that I was crazy for staying, you are right. If you think that I'm crazy for believing God and trusting Him for my breakthrough and deliverance, you are wrong. I am not sharing this so you can judge me or my former spouses, but I am sharing this so you can better understand what I had to walk through. Regardless what my former spouses did to me, I have forgiven them. So I ask you to do the same. As you read the book, I pray that you do not make the same mistakes that I made.

Remember that in order to gain with God, sometimes you have to give some things up. Keep in mind that the book is to help others as God has given it to me. It is especially to help those who are in a relationship and contemplating marriage.

Looking for love in all the wrong places can get you in a world of trouble. My first former spouse and I both went to college out of high school. However, we went to different colleges. Unfortunately, neither of us could seem to stay away from each other, so we both dropped out of college and got married. To tell you the truth, I should have gotten the marriage annulled two days later as I was abused on my wedding night.

He went into a jealous rage and physically beat me after he had given me permission to dance with one of his cousins at the wedding reception. He never demonstrated or showed the anger and other attitudes that he possessed until after I married him. I thought I was so much in love. I got married for all the wrong reasons.

I do thank God for our four wonderful boys from this marriage of 20 years. He was a good materialistic provider. He took care of the family, but when it came to love for God and me, he did not seem to understand what it was. I don't believe he knew how to love himself. You see, you first must know how to love God before you can love anyone else.

The Word of God says "Be ye not unequally yoke together with unbelievers; for what fellowship hath righteousness with unrighteousness? And what communion hath light with darkness?" (2 Corinthians 6:14). If you don't put God first in all you do you will be doomed for life. I'm not saying you have to be holier than thou, but I am saying that you need to know Jesus and be able to discern the tricks of the enemies. If you are thinking about getting married, make sure that he or she truly knows Jesus.

Go to God for yourself and talk to Him about your future mate. And then don't be anxious. Wait on Jesus to give you His answer, then do what He says.

Take it from me. You will mess up every time if you choose to lead your own life and make your own choices without consulting with God. The Word of God says, "Let all things be done decently and in order (1 Corinthians 14:40).

Now, like I said already my first husband was a very jealous man, but the major reason for his jealously was that he was a cheater and an alcoholic. Because he walked in a lot of deceit, he projected this upon my life. So he tried to buy me by giving me everything to cover up his own infidelities.

So, I decided I wanted to go back to college. I sat down and discussed it with him, and he was impressed and excited at the time and agreed to it. But despite his consent, he made my life a living hell. At that time he had money and so called earthly power, so, therefore he got away with lots of wrong doing.

I'm not trying to blame everything that was wrong in my marriage on my former spouse, but there were some things I went through with my first husband that others need to know, so they can be set free just in case they are in a similar situation. I was in a marriage for 20 years where I was physical and mentally abused almost on a daily basis. I did not fully understand what love really was. The wrong kind of love can blind you if you don't learn to love the right One first, and His name is JESUS in case you don't know.

As time passed the relationship became more and more strained. It seemed the more I tried to make the marriage work; both the physical and mental abuse became more prominent in the marriage. Looking back over the situation, I realized we allowed Satan to gain a foothold in our lives at the very beginning. First of all there were strongholds present in both of our lives. And because of this, this made it extremely hard to discern when the devil was fighting against us and our marriage. Let me tell you, if you don't put on the whole armor of God, you will not stand a chance against the devil.

Every attempt I made for us to pray and go to church together seemed as though it became more and more insignificant to him. You see, I could lift him up in prayer all I wanted to, but he still chose not to do it for himself. God doesn't make anyone come to Him.

However, my husband was raised going to church and to honor God. But, it seemed as though the more God blessed us, the worse he got. You know as I said earlier in the book, as long as things are going good in our lives, we go on like we are leading our own lives. But when things start messing up, we think about God only at that time. When it's good again, we go back to our old self. Well, God is not to be mocked or toyed with. He is not your "sugar daddy." He is God all by himself.

Take a look at these Testimonies:

We were at home one find day and my former spouse was in a rage due to alcohol. 'Til this day I don't even know what I did. We had three children at that time. He sat the children on the couch, got a gun and put it to my head and told them that he was going to kill their mother. Well, I didn't know a lot, but I remembered what to say. As he began to pull the trigger, I said to him in these words, "If you shoot me, I'm not going to die." He pulled the trigger and the bullet did not enter the chamber. He then threw the gun down and said, "You ..." (I will not repeat the words he said). "I'm tired of you prayin' on me" and threw my Bible against the wall. I thank God for saving me daily!!!!

I was at a friend's home playing cards and dominoes. I picked my mother up and she stayed at the house with the kids. My spouse was at work. I left and returned home at approximately 11:00 pm. When I pulled up my spouse had gotten off work early and was waiting outside. As soon as I drove up he pulled me from the car and started making false accusations. He then picked me up and slammed me on the ground and began kicking me. I believed that God quicken my mother's spirit and allowed her to come outside and stop him. Had she not come outside I feel as though I would be dead today.

You see if you are not walking in the fullness of God and you are doing everything under the sun, Satan will make you think foolish things. Jealousy is a dangerous thing. It will make you crazy if God is not the center of your life. Thank You Jesus for Your saving grace. I believe that my husband wanted to change, but the strongholds from Satan in his life made him do some unsettling things.

Now as I look back over my life, I can now better understand that through all the abuse, God understood that my cry for help was real and sincere in my heart. God understood that I had got myself entangled in a web and could not get out of it under my own strength. I did not truly know how to pray as I ought at that time. But God kept on acting as my Intercessor, for He knew my heart was in the right place. God also knew that even through all the abuse and pain that I was still committed to my wedding vows. You know, I learned that you cannot stop people from doing what they want to do. But I will tell you this; you are headed for destruction if you do not know Jesus.

The Bible says love covers a multitude of sin. (I Peter 4:8). Well, let me tell you; it really does. But at the same time I do not believe that God ordained for His people to live in Hell on earth by being abused physically, verbally, and mentally. I believed this type of mentality is ordained strictly from Satan as he tried to get me to give up on God.

Listen…when Satan knows that God is taking you from Realm to Realm and Glory-to-Glory in Him, he will have a tendency to remind you of your past. Listen, let me tell you what to say to that devil. For every time Satan tries to remind you of your pass, just simply remind him of his future. Remember "Job" in the Bible, how in his frustrations, he jumped to the conclusion that God was out to get him. Wrong assumptions; which lead to wrong conclusions. We dare not take our limited experiences and jump to conclusions about life in general. If you find yourself doubting God, remember that you don't have all the facts. God wants only the very best for our life.

Many people endure great pain, but ultimately they find some greater good that comes from it. All kind of people came to Job and reminded him of his past and of things he had and the things that they believed God had taken away. Even his wife tried to get Job to curse God and die.

When you are struggling, don't assume the worse. (Job 12:13-14). Even when you think you are going through your trials and struggles alone. Always keep in mind this promise, He will never leave you nor forsake you (Hebrews 11:5). Remember, this too shall pass. I believe that God spared my life, not once or twice, but more time than I care to count, so that I could help others as He did me.

First of all, I believed God knew that I believed in Him and loved Him in my heart; therefore God knew it was only going to be a matter of time before I totally surrender my will to Him. He kept on molding and shaping me. He knew He could eventually trust me to be one of his twenty-first century disciples for such a time as this. Through all the pain of mental, physical and verbal abuse, God kept strengthening me, so I could function and walk as one of His.

God strategically placed other Christians believers in my life to help me to fulfill my destiny. Through God's grace and strength I received a Bachelors of Science degree and worked in the school system for twelve years. And at God's leading, I resigned from teaching in 1994.

I'm reminded of two other very good friends that God placed in my life to travel with me down the dangerous highway to complete yet, two other Masters Degrees, one in Social Work and another in Criminal Justice. One of these friends has now gone on to be with the Lord. If she were still here she would say something to me like this, "You can do all things through Christ who strengthen you."

During the time I was suppose to pursue the Criminal Justice degree, I recall allowing folk to dictate to me what they thought I was supposing to be pursuing and not what God had ordained for my life. You see, we can allow folk to mess up God's plan and destiny for our lives if we are not in tune to Him. It's good to have college degrees, but if you don't have the real degree from Christ Jesus, you're still lost. The degree does not make you somebody, JESUS DOES. We have to pray without ceasing (1 Thessalonians 5:17).

But anyway, I decided to listen to myself and other folk and not listen to God. I ended up traveling to Louisiana Tech to pursue a PHD. In the process of doing my own thing, I once again witnessed how

God's extended His hand in my life. He saved me from death one more time.

Here is the testimony:

In the process of working on my PHD in 1994, I almost managed to kill myself. I was driving down I-20, returning from Louisiana Tech in Ruston, Louisiana at approximately 1:30 am in the wee morning hours and apparently fell asleep at the wheel. OH! by the way, I was driving a big Bronco at that time. Anyway, as the truck was rolling along, I was awakened by a loud bang crash type sound. Upon awakening, the truck was still on the road; the windshield was cracked and shattered beyond belief. The still voice of God came to me and said, "Be not afraid My child, for I have come that you have life and have it more abundantly" (John 10:10). He began speaking to me by saying, "My child you don't need a title to know who you are and Whose you are. I did not tell you to get a PHD, however I want you to get a degree in Criminal Justice." Thank you again Jesus!!

Even though I did not understand it all, I was obedient to God and went the next day to my professor and looked him square in the face and told him I was dropping out of the PHD program. He told me he was highly upset and asked me why. I recalled replying to him these words; "This is not what God has for my life at this time." He reminded me of how smart and intelligent I was and also provided many other reasons why I should complete the program. Listen, Satan will attempt to place all kinds of peoples in you life to abort your future. Now some believe they know what's best for you. Only God knows what is best for us all.

Well, I did not complete the program, but did follow God instructions. Remember, it is not about you, me, or anyone else. It is all about Christ Jesus. The Word of God says, "For God so loved the World that He gave His only begotten Son, that whosoever believeth in Him should not perish, but have everlasting life" (John 3:16).

Now I ask you the question, "Whom do you believe?" I pray that your response is God, because He is the only one that brought me through and out of my mess. And He can and will do the same for you. I say to you the readers, don't ever put your faith in people for they will let you down. Your only insurance is God. Only those things you do for Christ will last. The way to real **_JOY_** is to remember to put **_J_**esus first **_o_**thers second and **_y_**ourself last. God will give you Joy, unspeakable Joy that the world can't give you and therefore the world can't take it away — no matter what.

When it was time for me to graduate and participate in the actual graduation ceremony, I waited to find out and be directed as to which line I was to walk. The professor, who was the Dean over the PHD program when I dropped out, was now the Interim Dean of the College of Criminal Justice. He recognized me and called me over. He said to me now that I have completed this degree, I can finish my PHD degree. I said to him respectfully again, the answer remains the same.

Hey, I recognized that God spared my life for a

reason. You had better learn to ask God daily for discernment and to hear His voice in this fast paced, non-caring, chaotic world in which we live. Thank you Jesus for doing it again!!!!

I am reminded again, during my college years, of two of my favorite old one hundred hymnals. My grandmother and mother used to sing about "Father I stretch my hands to Thee, no other help I know, If Thou withdraw Thyself from me, oh! Whether shall I go?" The other one is, "I know I am a child of God."

Fellowshipping with other Christians in church is the best place to be especially when you are going through trials and tribulations. The Word of God says, "To forsake not the assembling of ourselves together with other" and that it is good to fellowship with other believers (Hebrews 10:25). God's Word also says, "To confess your faults one to another, that ye may be healed, the effectual fervent prayer of a righteous man availeth much" (James 5:16).

Now listen. Let's talk a minute about confessing your faults. Don't take my word for it. Let's go back to James 5:16. Confess your faults can be translated "confess your sins." Christ has made it possible for us to go directly to God for forgiveness, but confessing our sins to one another still has an important place in the life of the church. 1.) If we have sinned against an individual, we must ask him or her to forgive us. 2.) If our sin has affected the church, we must confess it publicly. 3.) If we need loving support as we struggle with a sin, we should confess it to those who are able to provide that support. 4.) If after confessing a private sin to God, we don't feel His forgiveness, we may wish to confess that sin to a fellow believer and hear him or her assure us of God's pardon. In Christ's kingdom every believer is a priest to others (1st Peter 2:9). We must help others come to Christ and tell them of Christ's forgiveness.

God's Word says to confess your faults to other believers in the body of Christ. Let me help you out before you make a big mistake and get hurt. We first need to ask God for discernment. so we will know who to confess our faults to. You see everyone in the church is not a believer. Surprised! Well don't be! Just believe that God's Word is true. Everyone who says "Lord! Lord!," will not enter the kingdom of heaven.

You have to remember that we have all kinds of people in the world. People are one of the reasons that keep us on our knees praying. Just as God uses His people to edify His kingdom, don't forget that Satan uses people as well and will use anything to get you to come to his side.

Let me tell you about some of the traps that Satan will use "to chew you up and spit you out." The first trap is something that I'm sure you're already familiar with is the love of money. The Word of God says that the love of money is the root of all evil. Make sure you get the scripture straight. It did not say you should not have money, it says what kind of trouble the love of money can get you into. Some other things Satan uses as traps are cars, men, and women. You see everything that looks good to you is not always good for you. Don't end up with the wrong thing because of what you believe you see. Looks are deceiving.

The Word of God says, "Now faith is the substance of things hoped for, the evidence of things not seen" (Hebrews 11:1). Satan comes to kill steal, and destroy. You know it is really amazing how Satan knows when you are at your lowest point in life and will single you out and use his schemes and tricks to beat you down and make you give up on life.

The Lord is good, and His mercy is everlasting; and His truth endureth to all generations (Psalm 100:5). The Lord wants His goodness to be a part of your life. Let me give you a bit of more good news to substantiate that God is just who He says He is. Let's do a quick recap. First, He spared my life, so He could use me for His glory. Not mine or yours. Second, God guided me through obtaining degrees and through all the trials and tribulations. By the way, just for your information and for the non-believers, through God's grace, love, mercy, chastening and my faith in Him, I acquired three degrees.

Even though I tarried a while out of God's will, He chastened me and pulled me back into His Will. God does not stop us from doing anything. He has given us free will or a choice to decide whom we will serve, God or mammon. God will also allow us to go through whatever we choose when we choose to lead our own life.

Now, to avoid any confusion, let me clarify something. Many people believe that they can continue in their sinful ways and just simply ask God for forgiveness and never repent. Well, I've got a news flash for you. Sure you can ask for forgiveness, and it is a good thing. But if you never repent, let me tell you, God will leave you to your own business, because you are saying to God "I don't need you. I can lead my own life and handle my own business. So God I'll just put you on the back burner for now until I need you again." I say to you readers that have this mentality, stop it now for you are destined for destruction.

There is a difference between forgiveness and repentance. Many of us, including myself at one time, have a tendency to purposefully ask God for forgiveness even though we know that we want to go back and commit that same sin again and again. I know, because I used it when I was gambling. I thought of every excuse in the book to keep doing it so I asked for forgiveness, cause after all, I knew the Word of God says that He is just to forgive you. You see we like to take God's Holy Scriptures and dress them up to suit what we are doing at that time. We want to avoid looking at the big picture. So to me, when you ask for forgiveness, this is just your way of using God, because you know you have plans to go back and do it again. You have no intentions of stopping it. True repentance means, "to turn away from."

Remember the story of how God chose Moses to lead His people out of bondage in Egypt. Well, anyway if you do, you will know how much God loved Israel as well. But it seemed that after they got what they wanted from God, they turned their back to Him and started serving and worshipping idols or false gods. As a result of this, God left them unattended and allowed them to walk in circles for 40 years. He never stopped loving them, but He turned His back on them because they were ungrateful and God gave them chance after chance after chance to turn from their wicked ways. So, don't think we are any better. I want to take the time to say, "Thank You Jesus for all the accomplishment that You entrusted me with. I believe that there are many more to come."

During the time that I was pursuing the last master's degree, I decided to get married again. Now notice I said "I" decided to get married. Again, I left God out of the plan. You see if God is not the center of your life; I don't care how much you have accomplished, you will still be lost for you see it is not about any of those things. It's all about Jesus. I thought since God had allowed me to accomplish this task that I was prepared for life. But life without God is no life at all. You see the devil can set you up just when you think you got it going on; take it from me. You see I have first hand experience. In other words "I been there", "seen that", and "done that" as some would say.

Now let's set the records straight. God is a forgiving God, a just God, an all-knowing God, a merciful God, a kind God, and a loving God. I just can't tell it all. However, I do not want you to miss the real deal... the target. God is not mocked. There is another side to God and He is not to be toyed with. Remember when God got angry with the moneychangers who had taken His sacred Tabernacle for a place of thieves? Again, do you remember when God used Moses to lead his children out of bondage from Egypt? Anyway, when they got what they wanted from God, they forgot all about Him and started worshipping Idol gods.

Isn't it just like us to think we can get what we want from God and then believe we can ditch Him or put Him on the backburner until our next crisis comes up? Even if we are saved, sanctified and filled with the Holy Ghost, we all are still guilty. I know. But it is one thing to recognize it and another to change your ways.

I know what you may be thinking. Okay the Word of God says we all fall short of His Glory. We will use this scripture until you run it in the ground just to make our selfish selves feel good. I've been there, seen that, and done all of that. But there comes a time that we need to grow up and real with God's Word. I'll tell you now that the only way to lasting success is through Christ Jesus.

I put myself through so much DRAMA before I actually understood that my ways had to be God's Ways or I would always fail. Now back to the DRAMA with Israel. Oh how God loved Him some Israel!! Even though God gave them warning after warning, and they believed that God loved them so much that they could do any sinful thing, instead of taking heed to

God's warnings they got worse instead of better. The reason I believe they did this was they simply forgot Who was really in charge of their lives. I also believed that they thought Moses was in charge and took their mind off the main source, our only true and living God, and that messed them up.

Now I know we all mess up, but do not be deceived by all you see and hear. For everything that sounds or looks good is not always the best thing for us even if it looks good to us. Remember we walk by faith and not by sight. To make a long story short, if you want to branch out on your own and do things your way and not God's Will then he will leave you unattended for that time. God wants to wash us clean from our sin. He wants us to clean up what we messed up and start our life over with Him always. Now remember, if God brought me out of it He can do the same for you, you and you if you only trust and believe in only Him and not man. God is able to do above all we ask or think, according to the power that works in us. The Lord will give you help and strength for work He bids you to do. All He asks of you is to serve Him from a heart of love.

There is a thing called "people pressure." The desire for approval of other makes us do strange things. We wear clothing that is fashionable whether we like it or not, we accept invitations we would rather decline, and we work much harder than we want to for a level of financial success we don't need. Worse of all, we sometimes choose to follow the so-called "in crowd" that encourages us to do wrong. In 1st Kings 12, we read about King Rehoboam, who also allowed "people pressure" to force him to do what they wanted him to do and not listen to the good advice of the older wise men that knew his father Solomon.

The wise men wanted Rehoboam to avoid the mistakes Solomon had made when he was king. Instead, Rehoboam listened to and was influenced by the counsel of his peers, such as the young advisors with whom he had grown up with. I would guess that they were also motivated by pride and a desire for power. But, oh how dearly we pay for our mistakes when we are led by others and not God. We are all influenced by "people pressures" in one way or another. It bears down on us from all directions. But we can choose the path we will take. If we are swayed by the proud or by those who love money, live for pleasure, or long for power, "people pressure" will lead us down a road of destruction. But if we heed the counsel of this who is humble, good and godly, we will follow the way that pleases God. Remember this…**THOSE WHO FOLLOW THE CROWD SOON BECOME PART OF THE CROWD.**

We all have a "But God" story. Let me tell you about mine. I can now say to Satan when he tries to bring up my old video, "Yeah I used to gamble at the racetrack and the casino seven days a week, but God brought me out. I once was diagnosed with cancer, but God healed me. I was once physically and mentally abused in my marriages, but God brought me out." Again I ask you…do you have a "But God" story? Remember only those things you do for Christ will last.

CHAPTER SIX

My Depression Years

One of the toughest times in my life was in 1997 when my mother went home to be with the Lord. Even though we all know that no one is going to live forever, but when death comes to your family, it has a way of paralyzing you. And how vicariously we quote the scripture in 2 Corinthians 5:8 for "to be absent from the body is to be present with the Lord." But during the death of mother I could have cared less for this scripture. I was so distraught that I felt completely numb. The only thing I FOCUSED ON WAS THAT I COULD NOT TALK TO, FEEL OR TOUCH MY MOTHER ANYMORE.

SHE WAS NO LONGER AVAILABE FOR OUR GIRL TALKS. I COULD NO LONGER GO TO HER AND TELL HER ABOUT WHAT I WAS FEELING OR WHO DID WHAT TO ME.

After my mother's death, life became a ritual for me. I would muster up just enough energy every-day to get to work on time. And when I reflect back over this period in my life, I realized that it was only because of my kids that I even did this. Because most of my days were spent crying and feeling sorry for myself. Working in a hospital added to my frus-tration even the more. If a patient died that day, I would leave work and go home more depressed. This went on for at least a year and a half. I would feel drained everyday. I find this quite ironic, though, be-cause up until then I had always thought that I could handle anything. It is amazing how crises have a way of defining who you really are. If someone would have asked me before this circumstance if I had strong faith, I would had emphatically said, "Yes." But actuality, I did not. This situation allowed me to see this. Because my faith was not strong, I did not grab hold to the promises of God immediately to bring me through this situation. God is always our comfort and source of strength when we go through tough times. The Bible says His yoke is easy and His burden is light. God wants to comfort His people.

Often when people are frustrated or unhappy in an area in their life, they have the tendency to compensate for that lack by getting involved in other things. Unfortunately, usually the behavior that is often picked up is one of a destructive nature. This is what happen to me. I began hanging out more and more at the racetrack and casinos hoping that this would replace what I thought was missing inside of me. However, no matter what I did, it did not fulfill the void that I was experiencing in my life.

Since this time, I realize God is the only one that can fulfill totally and give you lasting peace. He wants to pour upon our lives living waters daily. If we learn to drink from His fountain, we will never thirst again.

I had to learn through my depression that you can't come to God halfheartedly or should I say by going one half or three fourths of the way. We must be totally sold out to him. We can no longer play church, the church must be in us. Ultimately, we are the church. In other words, you can't go to church and "git your praise on" on Sundays and sin the rest of the week. Neither can you decide that you are going to "do right" during the daytime hours when everyone's watching and then at night, do whatever you want to do. Be not deceived! God is not mocked. He is an all-seeing and all-knowing God.

Let me remind you, God made us. He knows what we are going to do even before we do it. I know because I've been there. It took much chastening from God for me. God has a way of getting His will regardless of your behavior. He knows how to humble you.

One of the things I love about God is that He loves us unconditionally. He will never stop loving us or give up on us, but at the same time we can't take God for granted. Looking back over my life, I realize now that God was watching out for me. I am assured more than ever that if it had not being for mercy and grace, I would not be alive today.

Definitely, I know I would not have gotten the honor from God to write this book to   inspired and help others who have or are experiencing depression if He was not protecting me. I know now that depression is a demonic spirit that comes directly from the pit of hell.

During the time I was depressed, I put myself through so much. Remember pride goes before a fall and then afterward destruction. During the years I was depressed, I found myself trusting in man more than God. Even though I went to church every Sunday, the scriptures that were being preached, I did not fully trust or rely on them. I felt lost. I just couldn't understand how God could take my mother. She served and loved Him with all her heart. I wanted her to be with me a little while longer.

I am reminded again of how Satan "turned up the heat" during my time of depression. In hindsight it's very interesting to see how, all of a sudden, I got all kinds of invites from people to go to happy hours and to clubs even though they knew that I didn't drink. Even so, Satan didn't give up. He recognized what my weakness was and used it against me at my lowest point in life. Satan tempted me by dressing everything up to look so good. First he reminded me of how much money I used to win at the track and casinos. Then he told me that if I don't get out of the house and do something that I was going to go crazy. Also, I remember him saying that this would ease my pain and it would get my mind off of things and that God will not send me to Hell for gambling. But he failed to tell me the whole truth as he did Eve in the garden. It was very interesting that very few people told me that I needed to seek God for He is and was the only One that could help me.

Take a look at this testimony:

From 1997 to 1999 I was totally depressed. I went through the motions of caring for my children and going to work daily even though my heart was not in it. I did not care if I lived or died. I had to have a shot in my arm once a month because I could not move my arm to comb my hair or wash my body. I now know that Satan had a tight grip on me and his plan was to kill me. In 1999 I was at church and I passed out at the altar while during prayer. I do not remember anything that happened to me, but I could vaguely hear, like faraway voices, talking. During this time I recalled that my spirit left my body and went to heaven and I visited with the angels of the Lord in the form of St. Peter and my mother at the gate.

I recalled begging to get in and was turned down. They told me that I had much work to complete on earth and it was not my time. I could then feel my spirit returning to my body and when I awaken there was a doctor on each side. I recalled the one on the left saying to me that they thought I was dead. The one on the right believe me after I explain what had happened to me.

I could hear the Spirit of God saying to me, "Christ is risen from the dead and has become the first fruit of those who have fallen asleep." Christ's resurrection is the guarantee of our own resurrection.

Even after this out of body experience I still was depressed. So in 1999 I was listening to the radio and there was a pastor that had a 15 minutes broadcast that came on. I could feel the anointing from the radio as I was drawn to the teaching like a magnet. This man acknowledged himself as being a Prophet of God and stated that he was coming to the Bossier City area. Well, there was something inside of me that told me I needed to be in this particular meeting. And God did not let me down.

As I listened to the excerpts from the message I could feel the anointing upon the Word and it was as though I froze in my chair as God started speaking to me and told me that I would be attending this healing and blessing meeting in Bossier City. Well, I had tried everything else, so I said to myself why not try one last thing. Well, wouldn't you know that Satan tried everything to keep me away from that meeting. My car broke down, the tire went flat, and just all kinds of drama started happening the day this Prophet of God was scheduled to arrive. But God had a ram in the bush. Someone that owned a shop where I worked picked the car up and repaired it. THE TOTAL CAME TO $200, BUT I WAS ONLY CHARGED $8.00 FOR THE TOTAL CAR REPAIRS. Thank you Jesus!!!

Anyway as I told you earlier, I did much crying, but I did make it to the meeting. God spoke to me and said, "Hush my child everything is alright." I recalled drying my tears that night in 1999 at Bossier Civic Center in Bossier City, Louisiana where God sent one of his Prophets Pastor David Paul to heal me. That night Prophet Paul called out my mother's name and then my name and that is all I remembered. I passed out on the floor. The power of God overshadowed me. As he laid his hands on me I recalled feeling all the weight that was so heavily on me being lifted off. I felt as light as a feather. Every bit of the pain that I was experiencing left also. I felt renewed, restored and rejuvenated again. You see when you are all weighted down with the cares of the world and crying about everything, you cannot hear from God . If God had not intervened when the car broke down, I would have missed my healing blessing. Our God is bigger than all our problems. All you have to do is turn them over to God and He'll work them out. That night I was completely healed of the pain of my mother's death. God used a stranger to bring healing into my life.

If you seek God, you will find Him. (1st Chronicle 28:9)

- To find God we must be willing to seek him.

- It is required act of stewartship that one be found faithful. (1st Corinthians 4:2)

- God doesn't ask us to be successful, but He does ask us to be faithful.

- You are of more value than many sparrows. (Luke 12:7)

- Nobody wins when we play favorites.

- Lord, help me to love the way that You love.

- Help me to love the humble, the lowly the meek,

- And help me to care the way that You care for Sinners, the Weak and the Outcast.

I know God favored me because I know that there was no way in this world that I would still be here to write this book today and share my story. The good part is that I never stopped going to church, but I tell you I had some drama going on.

My sisters and brothers were there for me. I believed that I grew up in one of the best families in the world. If I had to choose my brothers and sisters all over again, I would choose the ones I have now. They were always supportive, giving me words of wisdom during the years I was depressed. They would call so much to check on me that it became an annoyance. I would get tired of trying to figure out what to say and what lie to tell them, so they would think that I was okay and stop calling me so much. All I wanted to do was just be by myself, and for everyone else in the world to leave me alone to die. I wanted so bad to be with my mother in heaven.

In fact I would even complain about my older brother Slim (as we affectionately call him) calling me so much. I had to be armed when he called. So I would prepare myself to sound like I was on top of the world. I could just about figure out when he was going to call, so I would get my script ready. But no matter what I said to discourage his continuous calling, he never stopped calling. And like each call before, He would always tell me to read Mark 11:22. He sounded like a broken record. He would go so far as to ask me if I had actually read it. I would lie and say yes just to get him off the phone. But I am so thankful that he did

But one day it finally dawned on me that it must be something special about this scripture that he keeps wanting and reminding me to read it. So, finally I picked up the Bible and read this scripture. Over and over again I read it. Guess what? I noticed the more I read it, the stronger and better I felt. So I read it until it became embedded in my spirit. Incidentally, because of my brother's persistence, I won a Bible and some other gifts from a radio station that I was listening to one day. The announcer was doing a Bible quiz trivia. The announcer stated that the first person to call and tell where the scripture (Mark 11:22) is found and recite it would win. Well I didn't even have to pick up the Bible. My brother had drilled it in my head so much. The announcer even asked the question as to how did I manage to find the scripture so fast? Of course, I told him it was because of my brother's persistence.

This was not the only incident that happened to me during my depression. I have a brother that lived in Pasadena, California. One day I was at work in Shreveport and he showed up citing that he just came to hang out with me for a week. I recalled thinking in my mind at that time that they really think that I have lost my mind. Satan can really mess with your mind especially when you are at your lowest and weakest point and living in darkness. Although I was happy that my brother took the time to come and see about me, his arrival made things a lot harder for me. Now I had to pretend even harder.

I was so happy when the day came that I was set free from the darkness of depression. I recalled being with a close friend in Houston, Texas visiting my family and we were at a restaurant when I told them that God had delivered me from the stronghold of depression. I recalled them taking a deep breath and thanking God and saying, "It's about time!" Thank You Jesus for I was getting tired. My family is the greatest!!!!

God showed me what my purpose and destiny were after He found that He could truly trust and depend on me to help others no matter what. I ask God daily to teach me to do His will. To keep me walking in His light, following His truth, obeying His word, not worrying about what I do or what I am or where I'm going, but desiring only His perfect will for my life.

Now I definitely want you to know this. I was one of those persons who believed that everyone that said they loved you, really did. This was a tremendous blind spot in my life because I would love people deeply. I have always had a genuine concern for other people's pain. And because of this I would take it upon myself to try and fix everybody's situation. I was a real "Ms. Try-to-fix-it-so-everyone-would-be-happy" person. But how many know this didn't work.

I thought I had so many friends. I gave and gave from my heart and I never even thought about it. But when I needed help, I never got anything back in return. I could not understand it. I began thinking that I must be doing something wrong. Eventually God showed me, however, that many of these people were in my life for what they could borrow and gain from me materialistically. But God saw that I did not understand fully, so He began moving these people from my life.

When God starts to elevate you in Him, you will find that you will have very few family and friends who fully understand this shift in your life. You would think that everybody would be excited and rejoice with you when God is moving in your life, but this is not always true.

As a matter of fact, the ones that said they loved me are ones that turned their backs on me. Now don't get me wrong. I don't regret that I helped them because it taught me a valuable lesson. And if I had to do it all over again, I would still help them, but I would do it differently. Satan can use people's needs to distract you from the real purpose or calling that God has upon your life. He would wear you out trying to take care of everybody needs.

However, when God began to move these people from my life, it was a very unpleasant experience for me. I thought I needed all these so-called friends. But God removed them all. God showed me that it was the best thing that ever happened to me. But God did, however, replace every one of the so-called friends with even better Christian friends.

God always have our back. He knew my heart and He knew because of my caring spirit that I would be taken advantage of. Regardless of what we go through, He will bring us out. What we have to do is ask Him to shape our character so that our character will match our destiny.

God always look at our hearts. King David did not do everything right, but it is said that God saw his heart.. We might not always do everything right, but if our hearts our pure and righteous about our actions, God will sustain us.

CHAPTER SEVEN

The 'Now' Years:
The Renewed Years

As I reflect and look back over my life, it's sometimes a little scary to see how God loved me so much that He brought me out of all my mess and drama. He washed me clean and gave me a fresh new start and for that I thank God 24-7 as some would say. God brought me through all the physical and verbal abuse as well as the depression years in my life. He did it so smoothly that I did not recognize where He was taking me.

I recall now how I would feel sorry for myself and my life. I now finally realized what God wanted to do in my life so long ago. He was just waiting for me to come to Him. God wants us even if we feel or believe otherwise. I know I was a mess. But God can take a mess and make a miracle out of it.

Whatever you might be going through or whatever is hindering you from totally surrendering to the Lordship of Jesus, I want you to know God still loves you and He wants the best for your life. He is ever-present to assist us. All He ask is that we totally surrender our will to His will.

Now, God knows He can trust me. He knows He doesn't have to make me do something, I willfully now surrender to His will. We can feel sorry for ourselves the rest of our days on earth or we can pick ourselves up and brush ourselves off and allow God to use us. I pray this book will help someone to decide to come to Jesus now and not later. My prayer is that souls would be saved and that all that I went through in my life, others would be spared from this degradation and pain.

Here is another testimony:

In June of 2001, a doctor looked at me and diagnosed me with cancer. I recall looking him square in the face and saying these words, "Well doctor, I don't know who's this so-called cancer belongs to, but it is not mine. When you touched my body to perform that test, I was healed in the name of Jesus for God was in your hands."

The doctor made a joke out of what I said to him and stated, "Oh my God Jan! Let me take Him to a nurse. I don't want to squish Him." I looked at him again and replied, "Don't worry doctor. You *can't* squish Him for He is every-where." "You have some powerful faith," said the doctor "but you **do** have cancer!" I told him that I choose to believe that God had already healed me.

With that he then proceeded to prescribe

seven different medications for me. I cried after leaving the doctor's office and began talking to God again. I could hear the soft whisper of God talking to me in the midst of my tears. He told me, "With My stripes you are healed." It was a personal promise from God to me. My tears dried instantly. I regained strength from God and then began calling my family members one by one. I recall telling them that I had something to tell them, but before doing so they needed to promise and agree, in faith, with me that I was healed and all I needed was their prayers and support.

They all agreed. In 2002 I received a clean bill of health from the doctor. But way before the doctor told me this, God had already confirmed with me that I was healed. Unfortunately, the doctor did not understand that God had already given me this in a prior report. I ask you today, "Whose report will you believe?" Are you going to believe the report of the doctor or are you going to believe the report of the Lord. Well, I chose to believe the report of the Lord. You see, the report of the doctor was a *fact,* but it was not the *truth.*

If you are struggling with some type of issue in your live right now, let me encourage you to turn it over to God and watch Him work. He is not the author of confusion. We are the ones that often put ourselves through unnecessary drama and then blame God for what happened even though we did not consult Him ahead of time.

God is concerned about every little detail of our life. Unlike man, God cares for us continually. During my depressed years and this cancer episode, I was on at least 7 different medications. But thanks be to God; He never failed me, not even once. Because of God's miraculous power, I am not on any of those medications now. I don't know about you, but I think this is a moment for a praise break — "Thank You, Jesus."

After God saw that He could really trust me and use me as one of his twenty-first century disciples, then and only then did He take me to the next level in Him. But with every new level in God, there are new devils and issues associated with it. All of which comes to defeat you and deter you from your destiny. But in spite of the devil and his demonic allies, God is teaching me to never give place to him and to never entertain him at any time; for he has no power over me until I relinquish it to him.. The Word of God says that the devil comes to steal, kill, and destroy (John 10:10). God has taught me that He is my everything and without Him I can do nothing.

This became an even more reality in the year 2003 when God challenged me to relocate to Texas

Here is the testimony:

In November of 2003, the Word of Lord came to me and said that I would move to Texas. Well I sat and talked with God and gave Him all the reasons why I shouldn't go, but He was giving me the reason why I should. As God and I continue to dialogue with each other, He told me that obedience is better than sacrifice.

Well, this was all I needed to hear. I then began to ask God how He wanted me to do it and what He wanted me to do with my possessions. I heard the Lord say, "Sell what I can and give the rest to the poor." Despite this, though, I felt strongly in my spirit that the majority would be given to the poor. As I started preparing for my new destination I received word from a pastor that he knew a family in need and he would help transport some of the goods. We loaded up both our trucks with all the items I planned to give away and then delivered them to needy families. I then resigned my job of 10 years.

Some might ask the question if this was hard. Yes, it was. Even though I loved the Lord at this time with all my heart, mind and soul, it was still hard. But I still had to do it. So, I was obedient and trusted Him to take care of me. There were so many things that I thought I was leaving behind. But God showed me I didn't actually leave anything behind because He was with me every step of the way. Anyway, my son and I packed up and left.

I have a brother in Arlington, Texas that helped me as much as God would allow him to; therefore, things were not as hard as they could have been. It was not my desire to live in Texas, and for the first two months there, I sought God about returning home. The only thing He would say is, "Your work here is not done." So, I left it alone and began seeking God for my purpose and destiny.

Even though Texas was not without its ups and downs, I witnessed to hundreds of peoples there proclaiming the Good News of our Savior. As months went by I started praying and delighting myself more in the Lord and interceding for others as I do to this day. As God helped me get my focus off of "self" I started devoting my time towards His hurting people. This is when God revealed to me the reason He had sent me to Texas, and to this day I call it a "faith move." It was only after the work was done that God started opening doors for my return to Louisiana. My son Korey was excited, for he knew that the move back meant that he would get to graduate with all his friends. Anyway to make a long story short, God revealed my purposed and destiny to me during my stay in Texas and then opened the door to a much better position back in Louisiana.

You know most of the time when we have been working on a job a long period of time, we sometimes can get into a comfort mode and we become afraid to step out on faith. I petition you today to step out on your faith. Don't miss what God has for you by listening to your flesh or others. If it's really from God and you know it; then go for it. To everything there is a season and mine has come. God has a season for all of us. Perhaps, your season have not come or perhaps, it has come and you are afraid to step out in faith. Don't be. When you are obedient to God in all things, you will reap benefits and rewards out of this obedient.

Yes, I was scared, but I took the plunge anyway. Ever since that day, God has been providing for all my needs. One of the inspired writers of the Word of God said that, "I have never seen the righteous forsaken, nor his seed begging for bread." This is the reason that even when the storms of life come and the raging winds blow in my life, I can still give God a hallelujah praise.

God did not promise that the journey would be easy, but He did promised that it would be worth it. I leave this question with you. Have you ever just paused and sat and thought about God's majesty and greatness? If you haven't please pause and do it right now.

I would also like to help you by leaving a few descriptions of God that helped me while I was reading the book of Psalms. I offer you these promises from God today and forever. Even if you are an alcoholic, a drug addict, a prostitute, a hater, a liar, a backslider, an adulteress, or a fornicator just to name a few, it's not too late to come to Jesus and repent of your sins. God is waiting for you for He says in His word that "I stand at the door, and knock and if any man hear my voice, and open the door, I will come in to him, and will sup with him, and he with Me" (Revelation 3:20). Now "ain't" that wonderful news? What more can we ask for?

Here are the scriptures:

The Lord is a shield, my confidence and my hope (Psalms 3:3)

My source of safety (Psalms 4:8)

The King (Psalms 5:2)

The Judge (Psalms 7:8

The Most High (Psalms 7:17)

My refuge (Psalms 9:9)

The helper of the fatherless (Psalm 10:14)

The King forever (Psalms 10:16)

The Righteous Lord (Psalms 11:7)

Today, I am a living testimony of the goodness of God. God is my strength, my rock, my fortress, my stronghold, my shepherd, my deliverer, my support, my Redeemer, my King of Glory, my Lord of Hosts, my God of Salvation, and my light and my Salvation.

He is my Lord of Truth, my help in times of troubles, and my King over all the Earth. I asked that you meditate on these things day and night and forever. If you are not praising and worshipping God in earnest daily, start today with some of the qualities above that brought me through. When God has brought you through much like he has done in my life, you can't ever praise God enough. Yes, some people will look at you crazy. But when they do just invite them to join in. Either they will or they won't, so don't worry about it. Just keep praying for them and keep lifting them up to Jesus. God guarantees result. The Word of God says if you are ashamed to own Him before men He will be ashamed to own you.

I thank God everyday of my life. I thank Him for bringing me through the pain, the battles, the spiritual warfare and much much more. Keep in mind that it is not about us and how we feel. It's all about Christ Jesus. He's interested in our love and commitment to Him. He'll take care of you and everything else.

One of my servant's prayers is that each of the readers sees and understands the plight of "How I Got Over." But just in case you read this book and you are still wondering how I got over, let me make it plain. Jesus is the one who brought me over. As my role model, Nan E. Turner sings the song on her latest CD of "How I Got Over." The song says, "My soul can't help but look back and wonder of how I got over." But thanks be to God, today, I don't have to wonder anymore. God is the reason I got over. God is good? We say it in the church this way, "GOD IS GOOD ALL THE TIME AND ALL THE TIME GOD IS GOOD!"

If you are reading this book and you are unsaved and out of fellowship with God and wants to get back into God's Will, here's a sinner's prayer you can pray. All you need to do is say it and have faith in what you said and watch it come to pass.

Father God,

It is written in Your Word that if I confess with my mouth that Jesus is Lord and believe in my heart that You have raised Him from the dead, I shall be saved. Therefore, Father God, I confess that Jesus is my Lord. I make him Lord of my life right now. I believe in my heart that You raised Jesus from the dead. I renounce my past life with Satan and close the door to any of his devices. I thank you for forgiving me for all my sins. Jesus is my Lord and I am a new creation. Old things are passed away, now all things become new.

In Jesus name AMEN

THE SPIRITUAL JOURNEY TO BE CONTINUED...